W

Festivals of the World

ARGENTINA

Gareth Stevens Publishing
MILWAUKEE

Written by
ARLENE FURLONG

Edited by
GERALDINE MESENAS

Designed by
LYNN CHIN

Picture research by
SUSAN JANE MANUEL

First published in North America in 1999 by
Gareth Stevens Publishing
1555 North RiverCenter Drive, Suite 201
Milwaukee, Wisconsin 53212 USA

For a free color catalog describing Gareth
Stevens' list of high-quality books and multimedia
programs, call
1-800-542-2595 (USA)
or 1-800-461-9120 (Canada).
Gareth Stevens Publishing's Fax: (414) 225-0377.

© **TIMES EDITIONS PTE LTD 1999**
Originated and designed by
Times Books International
an imprint of Times Editions Pte Ltd
Times Centre, 1 New Industrial Road
Singapore 536196
Printed in Malaysia

Library of Congress Cataloging-in-Publication Data:
Furlong, Arlene.
Argentina / by Arlene Furlong.
p. cm. — (Festivals of the world)
Includes bibliographical references and index.
Summary: Describes how the culture of Argentina
is reflected in its many festivals, including the
National Gaucho Festival, Carnival, and the
National Immigrant Festival.
ISBN 0-8368-2030-4 (lib. bdg.)
1. Festivals—Argentina—Juvenile literature.
2. Argentina—Social life and customs—Juvenile
literature. [1. Festivals—Argentina.
2. Holidays—Argentina. 3. Argentina—Social life
and customs.] I. Title. II. Series.
GT4831.A2F87   1999
394.26982—dc21   99-11999

1 2 3 4 5 6 7 8 9 03 02 01 00 99

CONTENTS

4 Where's Argentina?

6 When's the Fiesta?

8 National Immigrant Festival

12 National Gaucho Festival

16 Celebrating Music and Dance

20 The Virgin of Punta Corral

24 Carnival

26 Things For You To Do
★ Make a Cockade
★ Make Peach Licuado

32 Glossary and Index

It's Festival Time . . .

A festival is called a *fiesta* [fee-ESS-tah] in Argentina. Argentines celebrate many events with a fiesta. They have elaborate celebrations to remember saints, to honor old traditions, to recognize the different ethnic groups that make up their country, or just to have a good time! You probably have lots of reasons to celebrate, too. So, come join us. It's festival time in Argentina!

3

Where's Argentina?

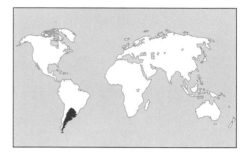

rgentina occupies most of the southern half of the South American continent. The country is very large, so its climate and landscape are very different from region to region, with deserts in the northwest and massive glaciers in the south.

Mount Aconcagua is part of the Andes mountain range in Argentina. It is the highest peak in South America, standing 22,834 feet (6,960 meters).

Who are the Argentines?

When Spanish explorers came to Argentina in 1516, there were many different Indian tribes living in the country. Today, Indians are a minority.

After 1850, immigrants came to Argentina from all over the world, because it was such a large and fertile land. Each group of immigrants brought their old customs to their new home. Most of them came from Europe, so almost 85 percent of Argentina's population is of European descent. As a result, Argentine culture has many European influences. The rest of the population is made up of Indians; *mestizos* [mes-TEE-zohs], or people of mixed Indian and European ancestry; and others.

This young Argentine girl enjoys taking care of her baby brother.

4

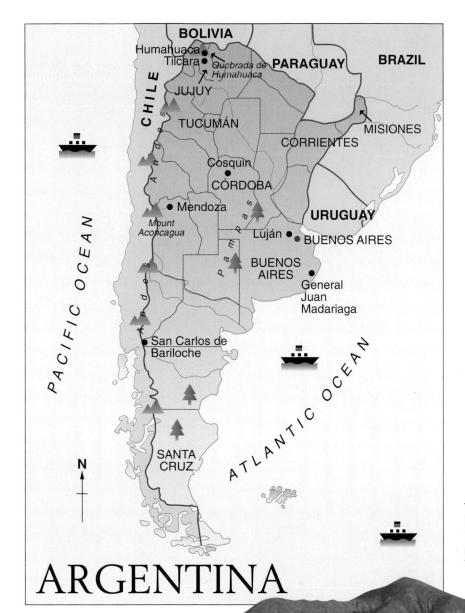

BOLIVIA

Humahuaca
Tilcara
Quebrada de Humahuaca

CHILE

JUJUY

TUCUMÁN

Andes

Cosquin

CÓRDOBA

Mendoza

Mount Aconcagua

Pampas

PACIFIC OCEAN

Andes

San Carlos de Bariloche

N

SANTA CRUZ

ATLANTIC OCEAN

PARAGUAY

BRAZIL

MISIONES

CORRIENTES

URUGUAY

Luján

BUENOS AIRES

BUENOS AIRES

General Juan Madariaga

ARGENTINA

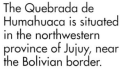

The Quebrada de Humahuaca is situated in the northwestern province of Jujuy, near the Bolivian border.

WHEN'S THE FIESTA?

C ountries, such as Argentina, that lie below the **equator** are in the Southern Hemisphere, where the seasons are opposite those in Northern Hemisphere countries, such as the United States and Canada. When it is summer in the United States, it is winter in Argentina.

Take a look at Argentina's many exciting festivals, filled with delicious food, soothing music, and colorful dances!

SPRING

✪ **NATIONAL IMMIGRANT FESTIVAL**
✪ **CHAMAMÉ DANCE FESTIVAL**—In Corrientes in October, people dance the *chamamé* [cha-ma-MAY] to celebrate their cultural **heritage**.
✪ **DAY OF TRADITION**—On November 10th, people celebrate their favorite traditions, and all cities hold fairs, with folk music and local foods.

SUMMER

✪ **NATIONAL GAUCHO FESTIVAL**
✪ **CHRISTMAS**—The birth of Jesus is remembered with images of the nativity scene set up throughout the country.
✪ **TANGO FESTIVAL**
✪ **NATIONAL FOLKLORE FESTIVAL**
✪ **NATIONAL PACHAMAMA FESTIVAL**—In the province of Tucumán, one of the oldest women is chosen to represent Pachamama (Mother Earth).
✪ **CARNIVAL**
✪ **NATIONAL VINTAGE FESTIVAL**—This festival celebrates Mendoza's wine harvests with parades, floats, and spectacular performances.

- **HOLY WEEK**—Religious processions are held throughout the country in April.
- **FESTIVAL OF THE VIRGIN OF PUNTA CORRAL**
- **REVOLUTION DAY**—On May 25th, the people of Buenos Aires celebrate the day the capital city gained independence from Spain in 1810. On this day, members of the Patricios

regimen, in traditional uniform, perform the historic "changing of the guards" in front of the Buenos Aires *cabildo* [cah-BEEL-do].

Do you like my Carnival costume? Turn to pages 24 and 25 to find out about the wild and wonderful Carnival celebration!

WINTER

- **SAINT JOHN'S DAY**—At midnight on June 23rd, the people in some cities build campfires and perform the traditional walk on embers.
- **INDEPENDENCE DAY**—In the provinces, mounted grenadiers and *gauchos* [GAH-oo-chos] parade through city streets to commemorate the United Provinces' declaration of independence on July 9, 1816.
- **SAINT JAMES'S DAY**—On July 25th, people honor the patron saint of cattle with ritual songs and dances. People also **brand** cows, sheep, and goats.
- **NATIONAL FESTIVAL OF SNOW**—This festival takes place in August in the snowcapped mountain region of San Carlos de Bariloche.
- **PILGRIMAGE TO LUJÁN**—People travel to the Chapel of the Virgin of Luján to honor Argentina's patron saint. Parades and exhibitions celebrating past legend and present devotion spill into the streets.

NATIONAL IMMIGRANT FESTIVAL

I n September, Argentines celebrate the National Immigrant Festival. Throughout the centuries, people from all over the world have come to Argentina and helped build the country. Because immigration is such an important part of Argentina's history, cities throughout the country organize festivals to remind people about the contributions other countries have made to Argentine culture.

Two young children wear the traditional costumes of their European ancestors for Argentina's National Immigrant Festival.

History of immigration

In the last century, many people from all over the world flocked to Argentina. Most of them came from European countries, such as Italy, England, Germany, Russia, and Holland. Others came from Australia, Canada, Syria, and Lebanon. In the late 1900s, new immigrants from Asia and from other South American countries arrived in Argentina. All these different groups of people have contributed a great deal to Argentine culture.

A home for every nation

During the first week of September, people in the province of
Misiones create a unique landscape. In a huge park, they build an
entire neighborhood of model houses from different countries.
These houses reflect different immigration trends that have
occurred throughout Argentina's history. There is a Swiss chalet,
an English manor, and an Italian villa, as well as typical houses
from Germany, Japan, and France. In fact, you can probably find
a typical house from the country of your own ancestors!

Inside, the houses are decorated just as they are in the
countries they represent. Typical music is played and traditional
foods are served. People go from house to house, tasting the
national foods and listening to the favorite music of people who
immigrated to Argentina.

A large and
elaborate model of
a typical Japanese
house is part of the
National Immigrant
Festival in the
province of Misiones.

NATIONAL GAUCHO FESTIVAL

S outh American cowboys are called gauchos. Early gauchos were mostly mestizos, people of mixed Indian and European ancestry. Each December, gauchos are honored in a special festival held in the city of General Juan Madariaga in Buenos Aires. For this festival, boys dress like gauchos in ponchos; baggy pants, called **bombachas** [bom-BAH-chas]; and leather boots. Girls wear long skirts and let their hair down to look like *chinas* [CHEE-nahs], or gauchos' wives. Parades of colorful floats and vintage cars let everyone know it's festival time!

A young gaucho learns the finer points of horsemanship.

The gaucho way

Gauchos enjoy singing and telling stories, so, during this festival, Argentines relive the gauchos' favorite pastimes with folk singing, dancing, and poetry recital parties throughout the city. In fact, months before the festival, contests are held all over the country to select the most talented singers, musicians, and **orators** for the main show.

A gaucho's life

Gauchos of the past caught and tamed wild horses, then used these horses to capture cattle on the flat, fertile plains of central Argentina, called the pampas. Gauchos captured cattle for food with *boleadoras* [bo-lay-ah-DOR-ahs], which are weapons made by tying three stones to the ends of long leather thongs. The stones wrapped around the legs of an animal and stopped the animal from running. In addition to boleadoras, the only other weapon a gaucho carried was a knife called a *facon* [fah-CON].

The gaucho way of life ended when the pampas was divided into estates, but many gaucho customs and values have been passed down to modern Argentines. The gaucho's strong character traits also have been depicted in art and literature.

Above: Modern gauchos work on cattle ranches. They are remarkable horsemen, and one of their main duties is "breaking in" wild horses.

A gaucho wears a *rastra* [RAHS-trah], a thick leather belt decorated with silver coins, around his waist. The number of coins indicates the gaucho's wealth. Notice the facon, or knife, tucked into the belt.

Horses, sortija, and pato

At the start of this festival, skilled horsemen perform daring feats that were everyday routines for gauchos. Breaking in horses and horse racing are some of the most spectacular to watch. Other exciting **equestrian** events include competitive gaucho games, such as the rodeo, *sortija* [sor-TEE-hah], and *pato* [PAH-to].

Sortija is a challenging gaucho game in which players approach a small ring hung from a high pole while riding their horses at full speed. When they reach the ring, they try to thread a pin through its center while still racing forward. When a player succeeds, there is much cheering and clapping.

Pato is a competitive team sport. *Pato* means "duck." Long ago, a duck was stuffed into a sack with only its head sticking out. Two teams of horsemen raced back and forth in the field, fighting over the sack. Today, a large ball with handles is used instead of an unlucky duck. The handles enable players to pass the ball to each other. Players score points when they manage to stuff the ball through a large hoop. This sport is very fast-paced and exciting. Everyone cheers for his or her favorite team.

A gaucho exhibits skill and bravery in the rodeo.

Eating gaucho-style

Gauchos had very little food to eat on the pampas, except meat, which they roasted over huge open fires. These barbecues came to be known as *asados* [ah-SAH-dos]. Argentines love asados, and they make the most of them by serving many cuts of meat.

People also savor a tea called *mate* [MAH-tay] during the festival. It is the gauchos' favorite beverage, usually passed between people as a gesture of friendship. The tea is packed into a special mate cup, and steaming water is poured over it.

For dessert, Argentines eat *tortafrita* [tor-tah-FREE-tah], a fried dough that children help prepare. At the festival, tortafrita is always sprinkled with powdered sugar. If you look closely at festivalgoers, you will find that almost everyone wears a little powdered sugar on his or her shirt or fingers!

These gauchos are preparing a cup of mate, a special type of tea made from the young leaves of the Brazilian holly.

Think about this

Gaucho customs have become part of everyday life for modern Argentines. Many of these customs and values were preserved through art and literature. The most famous gaucho is the legendary Martín Fierro, who has become a national hero. Stories about his life, his courage, and his code of honor are still retold around bonfires today.

CELEBRATING MUSIC AND DANCE

Argentines love music and dancing, and, throughout the year, they hold many music and dance festivals. One of the most important music festivals is the National Folklore Festival in Cosquin, Cordoba. This celebration, which is held during the second half of January each year, features the folk dances and music of Argentina.

Another important music festival is the Tango Festival, also held in January. Tango music is sometimes considered Argentina's national heritage. It is the music that most people associate with Argentina. As a dance, the tango is very graceful, with couples gliding to beautiful, **melancholy** tango rhythms. Read on to find out the highlights of Argentina's most important cultural events!

A festival is born

The people of Cosquin had originally decided to establish a folklore festival to promote tourism. The first Festival of Folklore was celebrated with nine days of music and dancing in January 1961. Gradually, the popularity of the festival grew, and, in 1963, the Argentine president declared it a national festival.

Today, its popularity has spread to foreign countries, and tourists flock to Cosquin to participate. Foreign musicians and dancers also perform in the festival.

This man is playing a *quena* [KAY-nah], a traditional Indian musical instrument.

Argentine folk dancers and musicians perform outdoors in the fresh air! These performances attract tourists.

The National Folklore Festival

About two weeks before the National Folklore Festival, contests are held throughout Argentina to find the most talented singers and dancers. The winners then perform during the festival, together with famous singers and dancers from Argentina and foreign countries. Besides folk dance and music, ballet performances and classical music have recently been added to the festival.

These schoolchildren in traditional costumes are ready for the audience.

Left: The tango is a graceful dance. A man and a woman hold each other and glide together in long, lingering steps.

Above: Charming tango paintings are found on the walls of La Boca, a district in Buenos Aires.

The origins of the tango

Argentina is famous throughout the world for tango music and dance. This beautiful music originated in the Argentine capital of Buenos Aires at the turn of the century.

Tango music is said to be a combination of the different musical styles of immigrants who settled in Buenos Aires. It combines the music of African slaves with the beautiful melodies of Andalusia, in Spain, and Southern Italy, mixed with the *milonga* [mee-long-AH], a dance that used to be popular in Argentina.

Tango music is played on guitars, violins, flutes, pianos, and *bandoneons* [BAN-doh-nay-ons], instruments similar to accordions.

Let's tango!

Although the tango was abandoned after World War II, and many old tango songs were lost, tango fever has returned. Tango dance classes have emerged all over Buenos Aires, attended by young and old Argentines, who want to learn their country's national dance. Argentina, after all, is known as the Land of the Tango!

During the first half of January, Argentina holds a Tango Festival. During the festival, tango musicians play melancholy tunes, as young tango dancers captivate the crowds with their grace. It's not long before members of the audience, young and old, start to do their own versions of the tango. Be warned—the beautiful, haunting sounds of the bandoneon remain with audience members long after the festival has ended.

Think about this

The most famous tango singer in Argentina was Carlos Gardel, who invented the tango song. Gardel popularized the tango in New York and Paris, bringing it worldwide fame. He later made recordings of his songs, which helped the tango reach a wider audience. When Gardel died in 1935, at the age of 54, all of Argentina mourned the loss of a national hero.

Many tango musicians are people who lived during the golden period of the tango before World War II.

THE VIRGIN OF PUNTA CORRAL

At the beginning of Easter week, an important religious pilgrimage, called the Festival of the Virgin of Punta Corral, starts in the little town of Tilcara in the Jujuy province. Thousands of pilgrims trek 30 miles (48 kilometers) through the Quebrada de Humahuaca to the **plateau** where the chapel of the Virgin of Punta Corral stands. Most of these pilgrims are poor Indians who travel many miles to Tilcara from surrounding areas. Indians from Bolivia and other South American countries also come to honor the Virgin.

Whole families of pilgrims make the long journey to Tilcara, carrying on their backs everything they need for a night's stay on the plateau.

A long way up

Many pilgrims start the long trek up the gorge of Humahuaca at night because it can get unbearably hot during the day. Whole families of pilgrims come, with some mothers carrying their babies on their backs. The pilgrims carry knapsacks filled with food, blankets, and other necessities for their overnight camp outside the chapel on the plateau.

The plateau on which the chapel of the Virgin of Punta Corral stands is situated at a height of over 10,000 feet (3,048 meters). Pilgrims reach the plateau only after walking more than nine hours, with only one short stop at the halfway point. At the plateau, pilgrims visit the chapel and pray before the image of the Virgin.

A mass is celebrated before the exhausted pilgrims break up and make camp for the night. They unpack their knapsacks, make simple beds with their blankets, and cook their meals around campfires. *Sikura* [see-KOO-rah] bands play through the night. The pilgrims will wake at dawn to start the second half of their journey, down the gorge and back to Tilcara.

The Festival of the Virgin of Punta Corral is an important religious pilgrimage in Argentina. Every year, thousands of pilgrims make the exhausting two-day trek up and down the gorge at Humahuaca. Here, pilgrims are stopping for a short rest at the halfway point up the gorge.

Tilcara's Easter Virgin

Early the next morning, the pilgrims gather outside the chapel for mass. A few women are selected to carry the image of the Virgin on the long journey back to Tilcara.

In Tilcara, tourists from all over the world have joined the townspeople as they wait for the return of the pilgrims and the holy image of the Virgin. In the evening, after more than ten hours, the exhausted but happy pilgrims finally return. They are greeted by excited townspeople. With the image of the Virgin of Punta Corral back in the church, Easter festivities can begin.

These women have been selected to carry the holy image of the Virgin of Punta Corral to Tilcara. It is a difficult task, but they carry it out with pride.

A shepherd's vision

In about 1800, a shepherd named Don Pablo Mendez saw a vision of a white lady with golden hair while he was tending his cattle.

The apparition commanded him to return the next day. He did as she requested, but she did not appear. Instead, Mendez found a stone resembling the lady at the spot where he last saw her.

He brought the stone to the priest, who rejected his story. People from the surrounding areas, however, began to climb to Punta Corral to pray to the Virgin and tell her their problems, making pledges and promises if she would answer their prayers.

Years later, the church finally recognized this miracle and built a simple chapel where Mendez saw the vision. Since then, more and more pilgrims have flocked to Tilcara to honor the Virgin of Punta Corral.

Pilgrims kneel before the holy statue of the Virgin and ask for her help as they tell her all their grievances.

Think about this
Although the Festival of the Virgin of Punta Corral is a Catholic pilgrimage, native Indian traditions have been added to it. Pilgrims often stop at stone altars, called *apachetas* [ah-pah-CHAY-tahs], along the way. They believe these stops will relieve their tiredness and protect them from any misfortune on the journey.

CARNIVAL

Argentines celebrate one last time before Lent, a season of **abstinence** and prayer, with a festival called Carnival. Carnival is held on the weekend (Friday, Saturday, and Sunday) before Ash Wednesday, which is the day Lent begins. During Carnival, people in many cities parade through the streets in colorful costumes and masks. The biggest Carnival celebrations in Argentina take place in the province of Corrientes.

A young musician gets the crowd moving.

Dancing in the streets

During Carnival, normal business and social life comes to a halt, and several roads are closed to traffic as everyone gathers on the streets to watch the parade of people in dazzling and colorful costumes. There is also a parade of floats. Some of these floats are elaborate creations that take months to complete.

Everyone is in high spirits, singing and dancing to rousing music and the beat of bass drums, or *bombos* [BOM-bohs].

The spectacular Carnival celebrations in Corrientes are so well-known that visitors from neighboring provinces and countries have flocked there in recent years to be part of the festivities. One year, there were as many as 80,000 people in the streets of Corrientes during the Carnival celebration!

Opposite: Beautiful, elaborate costumes dazzle the crowds during Carnival.

THINGS FOR YOU TO DO

In Argentina, one of the children's favorite games is *futbol* [FOOT-bohl]. When people talk about futbol in Argentina, they are talking about the game that many people know as soccer. Argentine children also like to pretend to be tough gauchos in Argentina's many festivals, such as the National Gaucho Festival.

Recite the gauchos' favorite poem

Pretend you're the plain-talking gaucho hero, Martín Fierro. Put on your baggiest pants and a pair of boots, and tie a scarf around your neck. Then gather around a make-believe bonfire in the park with your friends, also dressed as gauchos, and recite the gauchos' favorite poem about their carefree lifestyle:

And while some broke horses,
others went out in the country
and rounded up cattle,
and herded 'em together,
and so, without noticin' it,
the day went happily by.

Make a soccer ball

Argentine children often play soccer with homemade soccer balls. These balls work just as well as soccer balls bought in stores. Here's how to make one.

You will need an old sock—a man's sock would be best because of its size—and some old newspapers. Crumple the old newspapers into a large ball and stuff the balled-up newspapers into the foot of the sock. Squeeze the ball of papers as tightly into the foot of the sock as you can. Then twist the sock a few times so the ball is very tightly positioned in the foot. After a few twists, fold the top part of the sock over the foot of the sock that contains the ball of newspapers. Then twist the sock tightly, again, and fold it over the ball again. Repeat these steps until there is no more sock left to twist or fold over. If you twisted the sock tightly enough, your ball will even bounce!

Things to look for in your library

Argentina. (http://www.lonelyplanet.com/letters/sam/arg_pc.htm).
Argentina. Enchantment of the World (series). Martin Hintz (Children's Press, 1998).
Argentina: Land of Natural Wonder. (International Video Network, 1990).
Argentina: A Wild West Heritage. Marge and Bob Peterson (Dillon Press, 1997).
Buenos Aires. Cities of the World (series). Deborah Kent (Children's Press, 1998).
The Magic Bean Tree. Nancy Van Laan (Houghton Mifflin, 1998).
My Mama's Little Ranch on the Pampas. Maria Christina Brusca (Henry Holt, 1994).
On the Pampas. Maria Christina Brusca (Henry Holt, 1994).

MAKE A COCKADE

O n Argentina's patriotic holidays, many people wear a badgelike ornament, called a cockade, in the colors of the Argentine flag. The colors of the flag are the same as the sky—pale blue and white—to symbolize freedom. After you have made an Argentine cockade, you might want to make one in the colors of your own national flag!

You will need:

1. Ruler
2. Pale blue cardboard, 8.5" x 11" (21 x 28 cm)
3. White cardboard, 8.5" x 11" (21 x 28 cm)
4. Safety pin
5. Button, 1" (2.5 cm) across
6. Tape
7. Scissors
8. Compass
9. Pencil
10. Glue

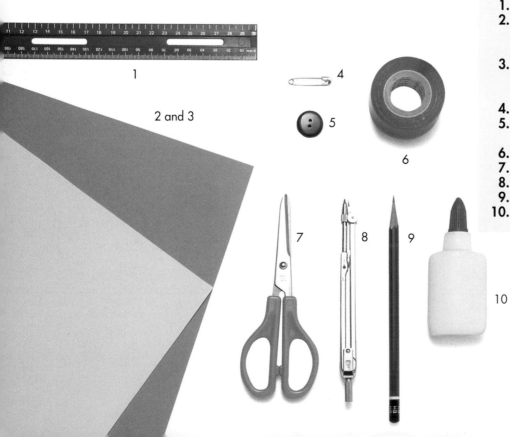

1

2 and 3

4

5

6

7   8   9

10

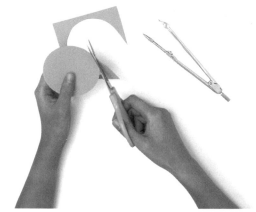

1 With the compass, draw a circle 2" (5 cm) across on the white cardboard and a circle 3" (7.5 cm) across on the blue cardboard. Cut out the two circles.

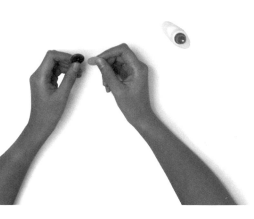

2 Draw two circles, each 1" (2.5 cm) across, on the blue cardboard and cut them out. Glue the circles on the front and back of the button.

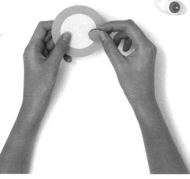

3 Glue the white circle to the center of the large blue circle. Then glue the covered button to the center of the white circle.

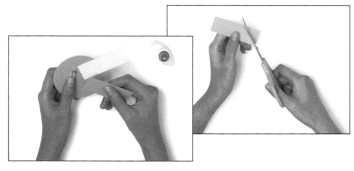

4 Draw and cut out two strips, 3" x 1" (7.5 x 2.5 cm), one from the blue cardboard and one from the white cardboard. Cut a "V" shape at one end of each strip. Tape the safety pin to the center of the large blue circle on the back side. Glue the two cardboard strips to the back of the large blue circle. Make sure that the V-shaped ends hang down close together.

MAKE PEACH LICUADO

Argentine children enjoy a beverage made with fruit, called a *licuado* [lee-CWAH-doh], more than any other drink. Favorite licuado flavors are peach and banana.

You will need:
1. Blender
2. Cutting board
3. 2 tablespoons sugar
4. 3 ripe peaches
5. 2 cups (480 milliliters) cold water
6. Measuring cup
7. Knife
8. Spoon
9. Measuring spoons

1 Have an adult help you peel the peaches with the knife. Cut the peaches into small pieces.

2 Spoon the pieces of peach into the blender.

3 Add the sugar and the cold water and blend until smooth. Pour the drink into a glass and add ice. Now you can enjoy a refreshing glass of Argentinian peach licuado!

GLOSSARY

abstinence, 24

The act of giving up food, drink, and other pleasures, especially for religious reasons.

bombachas, 12

Baggy pants worn by gauchos.

brand, 7

To put a permanent mark on the skin of an animal to show who owns the animal.

equator, 6

An imaginary line around Earth that is an equal distance from both the North and South Poles, dividing Earth into the Northern and Southern Hemispheres.

equestrian, 14

Related to horses and horseback riding.

heritage, 6

Qualities, traditions, and other features passed down from one generation to another.

melancholy, 16

Sad and solemn.

mestizos, 4

People of mixed Indian and European ancestry.

orators, 12

People who are skilled at public speaking.

plateau, 20

A wide area of flat land that rises high above the land around it.

INDEX

Buenos Aires, 7, 12, 18, 19

Carnival, 6, 7, 24
costumes, 7, 8, 10, 11, 17, 24
culture, 4, 8, 10, 11

dance, 6, 7, 11, 12, 16, 17, 18, 19, 24

Fierro, Martín, 15, 26
foods, 6, 9, 11, 13, 15, 21

gauchos, 7, 12–15, 26

horses, 12, 13, 14, 26

immigrants, 4, 8, 9, 18

mate, 15
mestizos, 4, 12
music, 6, 9, 10, 12, 16, 17, 18, 19, 24

National Folklore Festival, 6, 16–17
National Gaucho Festival, 6, 12, 14, 15, 26
National Immigrant Festival, 6, 8–11

pampas, 13, 15
parades, 6, 7, 10, 12, 24

tango, 16, 18, 19
Tango Festival, 6, 16, 19

Virgin of Punta Corral, 7, 20–23

Picture credits
A.N.A. Press Agency: 13 (top), 15; Asociacion Nucleadora Argentina de Fiestas: 8, 9, 10, 11; DDB Stock Photo: 5, 6, 17 (both), 18 (left), 22; P. R. De Andrea: 4, 7 (bottom); Victor Englebert: 1, 12, 28; Focus Team/Italy: 13 (bottom), 23, 24, 25; Eduardo Gil: 16, 20, 21, 27; Blaine Harrington: 3 (both), 7 (top), 19; David Simson: 14, 26; Trip Photographic Library: 2, 18 (right)

Digital scanning by Superskill Graphics Pte Ltd.